Mental Practice
and
Imagery
for Musicians

Mental Practice
and
Imagery
for Musicians

*a practical guide for
optimizing practice time,
enhancing performance,
and preventing injury*

by

Malva Susanne Freymuth, D.M.A.

Integrated Musician's Press

MENTAL PRACTICE AND IMAGERY FOR MUSICIANS

a practical guide for optimizing practice time, enhancing performance, and preventing injury

by Malva Susanne Freymuth

Cataloging-in-Publication Data

Freymuth, Malva Susanne.
    Mental Practice and Imagery for Musicians: a practical guide for optimizing practice time, enhancing performance, and preventing injury / Malva Susanne Freymuth
    114 pp.   14 x 21.5 cm.
    Includes bibliographical references and index
    ISBN 0-9670027-1-0
    1. Musical Instruments—Instruction and Study.
2. Practicing (music)—psychological aspects.
3. Practicing (music)—physiological aspects. 4. Music—Performance—psychological aspects. 5. Music Performance—physiological aspects. 6. Visualization.
    I. Title.
MT170.F74 1999
Library of Congress Catalog Card Number: 99-94063

Editor: Eleanor J. Crandall
Illustrator: Malva S. Freymuth.
Cover Design: Malva S. Freymuth.
Printer: CG Press

TABLE OF CONTENTS

Table of Contents, cont'd.

Table of Contents, cont'd.

Acknowledgements

My deepest gratitude goes to my parents, Karin and Peter, for their unflagging support over the years and for their help in creating some daylight hours in which to work on this manuscript. Endless thanks to my husband, Rick, for taking care of all the computer-related aspects and for helping me to make this dream a reality. Hugs and kisses for Benjamin who has been so consistently wonderful at bedtime, never waking to interrupt mom's late-night work at the computer.

Many thanks to the teachers who have had such a positive influence on me: Prof. Oswald Lehnert, Sr., my violin teacher and mentor of many years, for his inspiring musicianship, *joie de vivre*, and caring; Dr. Penny McCullagh for her excellence as a teacher and researcher in sports psychology, and for her interested support of my interdisciplinary efforts; Dr. William Kearns for opening my eyes to the philosophical aspects of music, and for greatly expanding my critical thinking and writing skills.

Much appreciation also goes to the friends and colleagues who so generously took time to read my manuscript and to give helpful comments: Alice Brandfonbrener, Barbara Conable, Grace Fuerst, William Kearns, Helene Grimaud, Julie Lyonn Lieberman, Mary Poole, Lori Saige, Sabine Schaffner, Gregory Walker.

Many thanks to Eleanor J. Crandall, editor, for putting the final polish on my manuscript.

Finally, I thank my violin for teaching me so much about myself and about life...

CHAPTER I

INTRODUCTION
AND
BACKGROUND

Did you know...

>...that mental practice goes far beyond just hearing a piece of music in your head?

>...that it is a skill that is useful during every stage of musical learning and in preparing for performance?

>...that mental practice has been the subject of much research and that its effectiveness is solidly supported by scientific evidence?

Often musicians develop some rudimentary mental practice skills on their own, but only a rare teacher will actually teach students to use these valuable skills. Unfortunately, few musicians realize what tremendous impact mental practice can have on their work and those who *are* interested often find that information on the technique is hard to come by.

A proliferation of research studies on mental practice can be found in the sports psychology literature, but unless you are motivated to do a lot of reading and independent thinking, these materials will not be immediately helpful.

To remedy the situation, this book focuses primarily on practical applications for musicians, while also providing some basic research background. Only a small portion of sources is specifically cited in the text. The bibliography lists sources that have played some role in shaping the ideas in this book and provides direction for further study of the research aspects.

Background

At this point a background sketch of my own work with the technique is in order. Over the course of many years, my tendency to "play music in my head" developed into a potent and multi-faceted practice strategy. I was initially motivated by a case of tendinitis that severely curtailed my physical practice time and forced me to find alternative means to maintain my musical skills. As a result, I learned that mental practice is far more than a last-ditch solution. It can also be used daily as a powerful technique for optimizing practice time, enhancing performance, and preventing musical injury.

• *Beginning Mental Practice Skills*

As a dedicated teen-age violinist, music continually occupied my mind. For example, I would mentally play through repertoire while walking through the beautiful foothills near my home. Music was on my mind during school too, and I'd tune out boring teachers by mentally "hearing" and "feeling" myself play. If a memory slip occurred, I'd simply pull out the printed music and use it for guidance. I also put in many hours of physical practice each day, often playing until hands and fingers ached.

• *Tendinitis Enters The Picture*

My intense practice habits and tendency to play with excessive muscular tension eventually caught up with me during preparations for an upcoming performance. At first I played through the sharp pains that were shooting through my hands and forearms, but three days before the performance the pain could no longer be ignored. The injury was clearly serious and required immediate rest. Desperate, I slathered my arms with liniment, put the music on its stand, and began practicing mentally.

Through this experience, I developed a variety of techniques for mental practice. I would imagine my ideal sound and recall the sensations of playing. I would mentally play along to various recordings of my repertoire. I would hum the music and mime the actions of playing. I would even dance to the music, moving my entire body in creative ways that somehow deepened my experience.

When the performance date arrived, I was ready and it was a success. And while there was still a lot of pain, I was amazed to find that I actually sounded better than *before* I took my enforced "vacation"!

Unfortunately, my initial bout with tendinitis wasn't harrowing enough to force a change in my overall practice habits. The experience taught me that developing a more relaxed instrumental technique would probably solve my problems, but I didn't want to take time away from learning new repertoire. Not surprisingly, tendinitis became a recurring fact of life and mental practice continued to be a stop-gap measure. I simply didn't know how to make mental practice an integral part of my daily musical work.

• *Debilitating Injury*

After a year in college, I attended a major music camp and festival. The competition was stiff and I felt driven to practice endlessly while ignoring painful signals from my hands and arms. What a mistake! I developed such a debilitating case of tendinitis that playing was out of the question. The pain had become so acute that I could hardly button my own shirt! Every task that required the use of either hand became an ordeal. My instrument stayed in its case and I abandoned my plans for a degree in violin performance. For my B.A. I wrote a thesis entitled, *A Summary Of Common Medical Problems Of Musicians, Their Treatment, And Their Prevention,* which reflected the things I had learned as a result of my injury.

• *The Long Rehabilitation Process*

Once the most acute stages of injury had passed, I began working with a physical therapist, a Rolfer, and a Rolfing Movement teacher, learning how to use my entire body in a more balanced and efficient manner. Over the course of many months, I developed healthy postural habits that would support the specialized movements needed in violin playing. While waiting for the pain to subside further, I read pedagogical treatises on violin playing, as well as numerous books on movement re-education, body work, and other methods of self improvement. I also set aside time each day for creative visualization and mental practice.

• *A Slow Return To Playing*

When I was finally able to pick up the violin again, I wanted to make the most of the precious few minutes I was actually able to play. By playing a few measures at a time and then practicing them mentally for several minutes, I was able to distribute five minutes of physical playing over an hour's worth concentrated mental work.

As I gradually increased my physical practice time by a few minutes each week, I placed the main emphasis on reworking my technique and learning to move efficiently. Another thesis paper reflected this process: *Violin Playing From The Perspective Of Mental Involvement And Physical Release.*

• *My Research Phase*

Once the combining of mental and physical practice had become an efficient habit, I began to wonder why mental practice worked so well. Were there ways of using it even more productively?

My quest for information led me to the disciplines of kinesiology and sports psychology which had generated a wealth of research on the subject of mental practice and imagery. I was able to further my knowledge by taking basic courses in kinesiology and researching the topic of mental practice for a graduate sports psychology course. I completed my research with a doctoral dissertation entitled, *The Application Of Sport Psychology Principles To Music Learning And Performance.*

• *Putting It All Together*

By applying what I had learned about mental practice to my own practice sessions, I developed specific strategies for supporting and increasing the efficiency of musical learning. For example, by alternating between mental and physical rehearsals, immediate goals were always clarified, and opportunities for analysis were plentiful. By mentally playing music just before physically playing it, my body was programmed to respond appropriately. Creative images, symbolizing certain qualities, further supported my technical and musical goals.

The general techniques set out in this book are the same as those that enabled me to perform the recitals required by my degree program, and then move on to playing professionally. (I also used mental strategies that specifically addressed violin playing.) Even today, mental rehearsals make up a sizable portion of my total practice time, and the benefits remain the same.

• *Teaching Others*

Once I began teaching my students how to use various facets of mental practice, I was surprised to find that even young students and beginners were able to respond to appropriate suggestions! In fact, players of *every skill level* can derive benefits from using mental practice strategies. To attain a high level of sophistication, however, mental skills must receive the same emphasis as scales and etudes.

In a teaching situation, mental strategies should be tried out and discussed *during* each lesson. Students need to provide sufficient feedback concerning the quality of their inner experiences so that the teacher can more effectively shape both the imaginal work and the related physical changes.

• *On Starting Mental Training*

The following chapters will discuss many ways in which mental practice and imagery can be applied. You're encouraged to experiment with the suggestions, altering them to suit yourself. You will probably find that mental strategies are easier to learn and use than they appear on paper.

Keep in mind that mental skills need practice and maintenance to retain their effectiveness. Count on spending extra time in the initial stages of training, and keep in mind that once you've built up "mental muscles" they can be used anytime, anywhere!

CHAPTER II

RUDIMENTARY
PRINCIPLES
OF
MENTAL PRACTICE

Throughout history, musicians have depended on some form of mental practice to help them achieve technical fluency and to refine their musical interpretations. One famous proponent of mental practice was violinist Fritz Kreisler. Renowned for his astonishing mental capacities and attendant disregard for physical practice, he wooed the world with his brilliant and soulful playing.

He would describe learning entire concertos while his violin remained in its case. Instead of practicing, he would silently study scores while on long train rides between concerts.[1] He felt that all technique was in the player's head and, as early as 1919, discussed the importance of creating "a mental picture...a sort of master record" of one's playing actions.[2]

Everything considered, Kreisler's abilities were extraordinary, and he probably had something akin to photographic memory. But even without such astonishing capacities, *every musician*—whether student, amateur, or professional—can learn mental practice skills to improve his or her musical work.

The Role Of Mental Practice

Mental practice is used as a supplement to physical practice, helping you to work more efficiently. By imagining how you want to sound and feel *before* physically playing the instrument, musical goals are clarified and the body is programmed to respond with accuracy and precision. By mentally reviewing your playing *after* the fact, your memory is exercised and long-term retention of essential elements is enhanced.

When mental rehearsals are regularly interspersed *throughout* physical practice sessions, the learning curve is accelerated and you are more likely to catch mistakes early. Furthermore, closely spaced mental rehearsals allow for the monitoring of fatigue and tension; this helps in reducing the chances of music-related injuries. You may still spend many hours working musically, but the amount of time spent on physical playing is somewhat reduced. In fact, more may actually be accomplished by a combination of mental and physical practice than is achieved when the entire time is spent playing. Sometimes, *"less is more."*

Mental Practice And Sensory Feedback

In creating mental representations* of physical events, you draw upon memories of physical sensations (hearing, moving, seeing, etc.). Because you have physically heard music, for example, you can imagine musical sounds. Having experienced the sensations of playing, you can recall these feelings and "relive" them. All the different aspects of a physical experience can be imagined, including moods and emotions.

Musical learning depends primarily on what you *hear* and *feel* while playing, with visual input playing a supportive role. As you develop mental practice skills, it may help to examine feedback from various senses—aural, kinesthetic, or visual—to identify which ones you can most easily imagine. Try calling up a few sense-specific representations. For example, can you imagine hearing a simple song? Can you recall the feeling of sitting down on a soft cushion and then standing up again? What about picturing someone you care about? Whichever sense seems most accessible may be the best

---

*In the research literature, the terms "imagery" and "imaging" are used in reference to *mental representations of all the various senses*. However, most people associate the term "imagery" with *visual* input only. In order to avoid confusion or misunderstanding, the various forms of "imagery" are always specified throughout this book (i.e. "kinesthetic representations," "visual images," etc.).

one to start mental training with. This way, you can gain confidence in your abilities before adding the more challenging senses. (Chapter III contains specific training exercises.)

Mental Recall And Mental Projection

Mental representations fall into one of two categories: "mental recall" and "mental projection".

Mental recall involves recreating an experience so that the mental representation is identical to the past event.

Mental projection is the creation of a mental "model" that embodies ideals that you strive for. As your music-making matures, these ideals may change.

• *Recall*

Mental recall always happens "after the fact." When something has been played very well, mental repetition of the experience helps to secure it in your memory. Recall of the experience also provides a model for excellent playing skills. On the other hand, if your playing needs improvement, mental recall is a means for analyzing difficulties and generating possible solutions.

• *Projection*

In contrast to mental recall, the projection of a mental model always *precedes* the physical event. It may be a representation of what you actually want to accomplish, or it can be a way to explore future options. When projecting a mental model just moments before playing, you are programming your nervous system and directly influencing the performance.

Projections also can be used to define intentions. For example, you can imagine what is to be accomplished during a practice session, or you can project more long-term goals.

When using mental projection in preparing for future events that contain unfamiliar elements, a mental model is created based both on personal experience and on information gathered from others. Naturally, the more experienced you are, the more detailed and useful the mental model will likely be. However, even novices benefit from contemplating situations outside of their own experience.

For example, to prepare for various performance settings, you might anticipate possible difficulties and mentally rehearse constructive responses: What kind of adjustment might the performance space require? Does the setting indicate a change in your typical stage presentation? Are there any logistical factors that might benefit from mental rehearsal? (If you don't have first-hand experience of a particular situation, seek out resources that might provide some of the information.)

25

The Basic Three-Step Practice Loop

In daily practice sessions, mental projection, physical practice, and mental recall can be combined into a simple three-step loop (fig. II-1). First, project an ideal mental model. Next, try to match the model with your physical playing. Then, recall and analyze this physical rendition. You can incorporate any helpful observations into the next mental model and repeat this sequence throughout your practice sessions.

Be aware that a mental review and analysis is not always necessary. Often, the changes needed become obvious even while playing. On the other hand, *projecting* a mental model is of inestimable value and should *not* be omitted. Intended changes should be clear in your mind *before* you try to play them physically.

Fig. II-1: Three-Step Practice Loop

Vividness, Accuracy, And Flexibility

Mental representations must be vivid and accurate in order to be effective: *they must fully correlate to their physical counterparts.*[3] In other words, mental representations need to reflect even the most subtle changes made in pursuit of musical excellence or they won't have the power to influence physical actions. In fact, if mental models are inaccurate, they can actually have a detrimental effect. Mental representations also need to remain flexible, changing in response to musical growth.

• *Vividness*

When practicing mentally, take note of any vague or blank aspects in your representations. For example, you may be able to imagine the sound of a particular phrase, but not be able to recall all the accompanying sensations of playing. To strengthen a mental representation, *increase your sensory awareness* during physical practice.

Try playing at a slower tempo, giving yourself extra time to register all the sensations. The mental recall should match the speed of your physical playing. Or, focus on specific aspects of the physical motions and then mentally rehearse each aspect. For example, a pianist or violinist might concentrate first on the motions of one hand, then the other, before trying to bring the two into simultaneous awareness.

• *Accuracy*

As the vividness of your mental representations improves, remain on the lookout for perceptions that might be distorted. If left uncorrected, they will be detrimental on both the mental and the physical levels. For example, a string player who perceives the fingerboard as being excessively long may consistently miscalculate shifts.

• *Flexibility*

In addition to being vivid and accurate, mental representations must be flexible. You must be able to alter your mental models to incorporate desirable changes. When working to change a deeply in-grained habit, for example, you may slip back into old patterns during mental rehearsals, just as you tend to do when playing physically. To remedy such a situation, mentally exaggerate those aspects that are to be relearned. Emphasize how the new patterns differ from the old manner of playing.

Balancing Mental And Physical Practice

The goal of practice, whether mental or phys-ical, is the cultivation of desirable habits and the elimination of undesirable ones. Of course, this requires enough physical repetition to train the neuromuscular system. When practicing something over and over, you can either string repetitions together or break them up with frequent, short rest periods.

In comparing these two practice strategies, researchers have found that the latter approach is far more efficient, that skills are learned much faster with a sufficient number of breaks between physical repetitions.[4] Frequent rest periods stave off fatigue and prevent a deterioration in attention. They also provide time to fully assimilate what has been learned.

• *Integrating Breaks Into The Practice Schedule*

Regularly alternating between mental and physical practice automatically creates many short breaks that allow the body to rest. To prevent memorizing subtle tension patterns along with the music, you should consciously relax your muscles while rehearsing mentally.

Complete relaxation provides a baseline of comparison for when playing is resumed. By repeatedly returning to a state of relaxation, a strong memory of these sensations is built up. Through heightened awareness, you also increase the likelihood that you will perceive excess muscular work when it occurs. Only by *perceiving* tension can you *release* tension. (See Appendix B for an overview of common relaxation techniques.)

In addition to the little breaks created by mental rehearsals, longer breaks need to be taken at regular intervals. These breaks should be introduced *before* sensations of strain or fatigue set in. This is a challenge, because as long as you are feeling good, you can see no reason to stop.

But consider this: muscles can be worked quite hard for a fairly long time-period *as long as frequent short breaks are taken.* The muscles will recover quickly and you can spend a reasonable amount of time on strenuous musical material. In contrast, if muscles are pushed to the point of fatigue before resting, they will take longer to recover and will tire more quickly when practicing is resumed.[5]

So, for optimum efficiency while practicing, take frequent breaks aside from the ones automatically provided by mental practice. To establish the habit of stopping before fatigue sets in, try setting a timer at 10-15 minute intervals. Take a few minutes off each time it rings, and then take a more extended break each hour. Use the time constructively, working mentally or doing some simple aerobic exercises, some stretching, and a bit of self-massage to keep the blood circulating and the muscles relaxed.

• Give Your Mind A Break Too

Just as the body needs sufficient rest, the mind needs time to rejuvenate and to gather insight and inspiration. Indeed, you often work your mind harder than your body during truly constructive practice sessions. Intense brainwork is needed during mental rehearsals and mental control is necessary during physical playing.

If your mind starts to wander, try changing your routine: practice a different piece, focus on some other aspect of technique, or even move to a different room. If this doesn't restore your interest, it's probably time to end the session.

Remember also to plan practice sessions before you begin, and to limit your goals in a logical way. However, remain flexible and change the plan if things are simply not working. If your concentration is off, try to analyze why and take steps to improve your frame of mind. When the session is over, evaluate your work and think about how the next practice session can build on or improve upon the one just completed.

Summary

Mental practice refers to the process of imagining experiences in a vivid and life-like manner, with the intention of influencing physical actions. When practicing mentally, you either recall sensory feedback precisely as it was experienced, or project a mental model that is based on personal experience but incorporates changes and/or new elements.

These two modes of mental practice (recall and projection) can be combined with physical practice to form a three-step loop. You imagine an ideal model of playing, and then try to match it with your physical playing. You follow this with a mental review that reinforces success and addresses problems.

Each mental rehearsal provides an opportunity for releasing tension. The feedback from relaxed muscles is incorporated into both your mental and physical rehearsals. Taking regular breaks is necessary and constructive.

Resting the mind is as important as resting the muscles for eventually both will tire. Reasonable goals should be set, and your mental and physical energy levels need to be monitored. If necessary, breaks can be taken or practice procedures can be changed to maintain mental focus and interest.

CHAPTER III

BASIC TRAINING
OF
MENTAL PRACTICE
SKILLS

Effective mental practice depends upon a high level of sensory awareness. The more conscious you are of sensory feedback *while playing*, the more clearly you can imagine playing. In turn, the more vivid the mental work becomes, the more powerfully it can influence playing and performance. This chapter presents a basic program for training mental practice skills and offers suggestions for heightening sensory awareness and for developing effective mental representations. The use of creative imagery is introduced here as well.

Keep in mind that different techniques and images may vary in effectiveness, depending upon the individual and that the training exercises are meant as guidelines only. If a particular exercise doesn't seem to work, try to understand the concept and then modify the exercise to fit your own needs and abilities. Be persistent—as with any skill, practice makes perfect!

Adjust the Workspace

When practicing, whether mentally or physically, be sure that the surroundings are conducive to good work and are free from distracting elements. In the interest of preventing injury while practicing physically, consider lighting, temperature, clothing, and hydration (drinking enough water helps both brain and muscles to function well). Also take into account psychological aspects; your practice time will be more enjoyable and your motivation to work will be greater if the workspace is pleasant.

Your own special equipment can improve less than desirable practice areas. Bring along a foam workout pad for stretching or lying down on during breaks and while working mentally. You might also want a portable fan/heater, a stand light, and ear plugs (it's nearly impossible to practice mentally if someone is playing loudly right next door). Inspiring objects of beauty (pictures and brightly-colored cloths are easy to pack) can make a sur-prising difference when a practice space is barren and uninviting.

General Considerations

Postural alignment is a fundamental aspect of playing an instrument and should be monitored throughout practice sessions. Properly aligning the body allows all the postural muscles to work in a balanced manner, which provides vital support for those muscles involved in playing the instrument. In comparison, faulty alignment causes some muscles to overwork, while essentially putting others out of a job. Over time such imbalance may well lead to pain and injury.

Most people need some help in developing healthy skeletal alignment and body use. While much can be accomplished through studying books on movement education, the guidance of a trained expert is indispensable. Consider working with a movement teacher using one of the following methods: Rolfing Movement, Aston Patterning, Alexander Technique, Feldenkrais Technique, or the Pilates Method.

Along with maintaining postural awareness, attend to your breathing and allow it to remain full and easy. Many people find themselves either restricting their breath or even holding it momentarily during emotionally intense or technically difficult music. Such disturbances in breathing may also happen while you imagine yourself playing. Remember that when working mentally, your overall physical state can be memorized along with the specific sensations you focus on at any one time.

When beginning mental training, pace yourself by employing only a few minutes of mental work at a time. It is also useful to periodically revisit the materials covered in this book. After gaining personal experience with the techniques, you will likely find subtleties on subsequent readings that weren't apparent before.

Training The Mental Representation Of The Five Senses

Visual Representations

Visual recall can be practiced by first looking at something, then closing your eyes and recreating everything you've just seen. Alternate looking and visualizing, deepening your perception of detail with every repetition. Some suggestions follow:

• *Printed Music*

Try visualizing a musical staff and imagine writing in a simple melody or some chords. Or, practice looking at some printed music and then reproducing it on your mental "screen." Start with a few notes, then try recreating the look of a measure or two. Imagine writing out a few phrases, and then move on to recalling the overall impression of an entire page.

Focusing purely on how the printed music looks is helpful in developing visual memory. However, this exercise is more useful if you can

also imagine the *sound* of the notes being visual-
ized, and the *feeling* of playing them on your instrument.

• *Your Instrument*

Spend some time examining your instrument.
Turn it this way and that (or walk around it if it's
large), and appreciate the variations in color, shape,
and texture, noticing too how light reflects off of the
different surfaces. Now close your eyes and recall
all of this visual information.

• *Yourself, While Playing*

Physically get into playing position and focus
on what you see of yourself in relation to your
instrument: can you see a portion of your arms?
What about hands and fingers? How do they look
when in contact with the instrument? To what
degree do you need to use peripheral vision?

Now close your eyes and maintain a mental
image of what you saw. Open your eyes again: try
playing something simple while remaining acutely
aware of all visual feedback. Stop playing and
visualize the sequence. With practice, this can even
be done with your eyes open.

When visualizing, you will most likely end up
recalling the sounds and feelings of playing as well,
making the imagery-sequence more vivid and
complete. This is actually what you *want* to achieve.
Just be sure that the visual images don't lose their
accuracy when other senses are represented.

• *Your Surroundings*

While you imagine playing, broaden the perspective to include your surroundings. Try visualizing a number of different musical settings such as playing alone in a particular space or being part of an ensemble. "See" your colleagues or "watch" the conductor, depending on the situation.

• *An Objective Viewpoint*

Practice seeing yourself from an external viewpoint. Try looking into a mirror, swiveling around to watch your playing from different angles. Or have someone videotape you from various angles. Choose contrasting pieces of music and focus on how your movements change with each piece. All these impressions can then be recreated mentally, as if watching a movie in your mind's eye.

It can also help to manipulate the images while you visualize. For example, try "zooming" in on those areas of your body that are particularly relevant in performing a certain technique.

Aural Representations

The ability to imagine musical sounds depends on the development of the "inner ear." Alternating continually between mental and physical playing is the key to building a strong musical memory, where aural representations are as clearly perceived as their physical counterparts. Below are some suggestions for isolating various musical elements and practicing them mentally. As soon as possible, bring these elements back together in their original context.

• *Memorize A-440*

To begin with, if you don't naturally possess perfect pitch, you'll want to strengthen your sense of relative pitch, practicing intervals both physically and mentally. One useful strategy is first to internalize a single pitch so that you can recall it instantly (and accurately). Then, use this pitch as a home base from which to find all other pitches. Since most instruments and ensembles tune to A-440, this is a logical pitch to choose.

In order to memorize this "home" pitch, begin by playing it on your instrument. Then stop playing and let your imagination take over, creating an unbroken continuation of the pitch with no changes in timbre or dynamic level (fig. III-1).

Fig. III-1: Memorizing "A"

This sequence will need repeated practice over a period of several days or weeks, perhaps even longer. The more often you practice it, the sooner you'll be able to imagine the pitch "out of thin air," dispensing with the initial physical prompt.

As the home pitch becomes memorized, keep reinforcing it. Carry a tuning-fork or pitch-pipe with you and check the accuracy of your memory many times per day. Mentally project the pitch *first*, then check its accuracy.

You might also *sing* the imagined pitch before checking it. (This is an intermediate step between the mental version and its physical counterpart.) If your internal representation is inaccurate, hearing it physically through singing, *before* comparing it to an outside source, can help to clarify the amount of correction necessary. (Naturally, this strategy only works if you vocalize well.)

• *"Hearing" Intervals*

Practice playing (or singing) and then mentally hearing all intervals within a one-octave range. Next be sure that you can imagine your "home pitch" in at least four different octaves (again checking it on your instrument).

Practice hearing intervals within each of these octaves, still in relation to your securely memorized "home" pitch. Finally try mentally transposing the intervals themselves up and down by several octaves, continuing to check your mental versions with their physical counterparts (fig. III-2).

Fig. III-2: Projecting Intervals

play   imagine   play   imagine

• *"Hearing" Melody, Harmony, And Rhythm*

When you can accurately imagine the sound of all intervals, begin mentally practicing melodies, chords, and harmonic changes. Beginning with very simple forms, mentally practice each musical aspect separately from the others. Then as your inner ear develops, gradually combine the different musical elements and increase their complexity. As always, alternate between inner hearing and physical playing to check the accuracy of your mental representations and to reinforce your memory.

• *Example:*

• Start by imagining the melody of "Twinkle, Twinkle, Little Star." Be sure that you can imagine all the pitches accurately and in tempo.

• Imagine the melody again, focusing on various musical nuances. Imagine changes in phrasing, articulation, tempo, vibrato, etc.

• Practice internally hearing a simple accompaniment of I, IV, and V chords. Imagine the chord sounds in their various inversions and also as arpeggiated figures.

• Make up various rhythmic figures for the melody or the accompaniment. Complex rhythms can be imagined on a single pitch, for practice purposes, as well as in their musical context.

- Finally, combine the different musical elements, creating a number of variations on the simple theme. With each of the above steps, remember to play musically and to practice *imagining* the interpretive subtleties.

• *An Exercised For Continuous Inner Hearing*

Try alternating physical and mental playing as you go through a particular composition. Maintain the musical flow as you physically play the first measure or phrase, then imagine the second measure (or phrase), play the third, imagine the fourth, and so on. An analogy could be made to playing along with a recording where, every time you stop playing physically, you hear the music continue on uninterrupted.

Kinesthetic And Tactile Representations

The kinesthetic sense involves perceptions of balance and movement and informs you about the size and relative positions of body parts. The tactile sense relays information about physical contact with the world around you. Acute awareness of how you move and use your body is essential, both in developing an efficient instrumental technique and in projecting vivid and accurate mental representations.

The three exercises outlined below suggest a possible progression for increasing sensitivity and for practicing movements mentally. If you are interested in pursuing more specific exercises, a good source is *Listening To The Body*, by R. Masters and J. Houston.

To get the most out of the following exercises, take a look at some anatomy books and get a feel for the structure of your body—*many people have misconceptions about their anatomy that adversely affect their ability to perceive and interpret their bodily sensations.*

Initially it may be helpful to have someone else guide you through the exercises, reading out loud. This way you can focus completely on the sensations in your body without the distraction of referring to the printed page. Another option is to read the instructions into a tape recorder and use the recording as a guide.

Exercise 1
Whole-Body Scan:
• Lie down on your back and close your eyes. Take a deep breath, then blow it out, tuning in to how you feel and releasing as much tension with the exhale as possible. Repeat this several times.

• Attend to the sensations in your body. Focus on your back and try to sense your spine. Try *gently* moving your spine back and forth on the floor, as if it were a snake. The motion should be very subtle. Let your arms and legs move subtly as well, and very slightly wiggle your fingers and toes. Imagine that you are floating in a comforting, warm ocean with little waves rocking and caressing you (or come up with some other relaxing scenario). After a while let the motions subside and enjoy resting quietly.

• Begin systematically focusing on specific areas of your body, releasing any tension with *very* subtle, gentle movements and relaxing images:

> For example, focus entirely on the sensations in your feet and toes. Wiggle them gently, attending fully to the sensations, and use creative images to help you relax further (i.e. warm sunshine melting away tension).

> Move your attention to your ankles (continuing to use subtle motions and imagery). Next sense the relaxation in your calves and lower legs, then in your knee joints, and so on through your entire body, ending with your head. Don't forget about your spine, scalp, and facial muscles.

> Try using verbal directives as you go along. While focusing on a specific area of tension, try gently saying (or thinking) words such as "release," "open," "flow," etc., to help let go of tightness.

• Tune in to the subtle sensations of your heartbeat and your breath. Sense how your breathing is a distinctly three-dimensional activity, creating subtle motions in your abdomen, back, and ribcage. As long as no tension is inhibiting your breathing, you can feel your torso expanding in all directions to some degree.

• *Notes:*
The above exercise can also be done in a sitting position. In this case, it's most effective to start at the top of your head and work your way down, imagining that the pull of the earth's gravity is drawing all the tension out of your body and into the ground.

As you become adept at relaxing systematically, you can keep tension from accumulating over a practice session. During breaks quickly scan your body, lingering in any areas that feel tense. If simple awareness isn't enough to dispel the tightness, use gentle movements, relaxing images, and verbal directives as needed. As your body awareness and control improves, you will also be able to release tension quickly while playing your instrument.

Exercise 2
Imagining Movements:

• Lying on your back begin with the body scan as described in Exercise 1. Then with eyes closed *slowly* lift one arm until it is perpendicular to the floor. As you move, attend fully to the sensations in your shoulder joint and in all the muscles surrounding it.

• Can you sense which muscles are doing most of the work? Are you tightening muscles that aren't actually needed in completing the motion? Raise and lower your arm several more times, consciously relaxing those muscles that are becoming needlessly engaged during the motion.

• Rest your arm and only *imagine* the motions of raising and lowering. Alternate between physically moving your arm and mentally recreating the motion.

• Next do several arm lifts in succession, making each motion sequence faster than the one before. Sense how certain muscles now need to work harder, while others are somewhat relieved of work. For example, in raising your arm at a fast speed, the responsible muscles have to contract much more strongly and quickly than when the arm is raised slowly. When quickly lowering the arm you essentially let the arm drop of its own weight, only "catching" it just before it reaches the floor. In comparison, when lowering the arm slowly the muscles have to sustain the full weight of the arm throughout the entire movement.

• Rest your arm and imagine the *quick* action of raising and lowering. Focus on the overall flow of the motion. Now, imagine the action at a *slow* speed. Although this version will include more detailed and specific muscular sensations, keep your focus on the overall flow of the movement (this type of focus is important when mentally rehearsing slow music).

• Try using a creative image to support the arm-lifting motion. While raising your arm focus entirely on the following: imagine a powerful jet of water shooting out from your shoulder, through the fingertips, and continuing on out to spray the wall and ceiling as your arm moves up (pretend that the arm is a fire hose dousing some far-off flames).

• Try focusing on the creative image during both slow and fast arm lifts. Does your arm feel any stronger or lighter than before? Many people report sensations of increased strength, ease, or smoothness of motion when using an image designed to facilitate movement. (See *Human Movement Potential: Its Ideokinetic Facilitation* by L. Sweigard, for an in-depth analysis of how creative imagery facilitates movement, and for many imagery examples. This book also includes discussions of the mechanical and anatomical components of movement.)

• Using the steps outlined above try other simple movements, exploring your body's range of motion. As your mental representations improve, increase the complexity of the movements and begin linking them into sequences.

Exercise 3
Imagine Playing Your Instrument:

• Begin by standing or sitting as you would in playing your instrument. Position yourself as if the instrument were present and try miming some of the basic motions involved in playing. Imagine the feel of your instrument as it contacts your skin and imagine how it would sound if you were actually playing.

• Mime playing some scales and arpeggios and mime playing through a few musical passages. If necessary pick up your instrument and actually play it to check the accuracy of your miming motions and to reinforce your inner hearing.

• While miming scan your body, releasing any tension and heightening your awareness of working muscles. Explore creative images that might enhance your movements.

• If while miming you can clearly imagine the sound of your music, try rehearsing purely mentally (without the "prompt" of the miming motions). Sit or stand quietly as you imagine both the sound *and* the feel of playing.

• If at any time you have difficulty recalling the physical sensations of playing or the sounds of your music, return to *physically* playing. Attend carefully to those aspects that were vague in your memory and use this sensory feedback to strengthen your mental representations.

Representations Of Smell And Taste

While these two senses are not specifically called upon when playing an instrument, they can be a surprisingly vivid part of recalling an experience. In particular we tend to form strong associations with smells and can use these to help recall certain performances or events.

For example, while mentally reviewing a performance you may find that you can remember certain smells. Perhaps there were fragrant flowers in the dressing room, or the air backstage smelled musty, or you got a whiff of rosin dust. Imagining scents, along with all the other aspects of an experience, makes the recall more vivid and real.

• *Use Scents To Influence Mood*

Try diffusing fragrant oils in your practice room, using specific scents to influence your mood. For example, the scent of lavender is known to be calming, while rosemary is rejuvenating and vanilla is comforting. (There are dozens of essential oils to choose from and most suppliers have printed materials outlining the therapeutic effects of each scent.) Experiment with using scents while performing as well, and see whether physically smelling the scent later on helps to trigger your memory of the performance.

• *Completing The Picture*

Taste is the most incidental sense in recalling a musical experience. However, if you eat or drink something particular just before performing, recalling the taste may add a finishing touch to your mental depiction of an event.

Closing Comments

The mental practice and imagery exercises outlined in this chapter are meant as starting points. They certainly are not the only way of approaching training. Most likely you will have personal revelations that expand on the materials presented here. More power to you! Above all remember to enjoy the learning process. If negative feelings arise, take a break!

CHAPTER IV

WHY AND HOW DOES MENTAL PRACTICE WORK?

The influence of mental practice on physical learning and performance has thus far been investigated in approximately 200 research studies. Because any one study can only examine a small portion of mental practice effects, a comprehensive review of the literature was conducted in 1983. The purpose of this review was to summarize all the statistically significant findings contained in the research.[6]

The "meta-analysis" approach was used, which involved taking the results of all the studies and putting them through a series of statistical analyses. Questionable or insignificant results were weeded out, while findings substantiated by an appropriate number of studies were identified.

The review delineated the underlying reasons mental practice works and gave general guidelines for using mental practice. Mental practice effects were grouped into four primary categories: 1) cognitive aspects, 2) stages of learning, 3) physiological effects, and 4) pre-performance strategies. Essential points of the review will be discussed below, along with practical suggestions for applying the research findings in a musical setting.

Category 1:
Strategies For Reinforcing
Cognitive Aspects Of A Skill

Physical skills can be categorized along a continuum ranging from very simple to very complex. The more complex a skill is, the more intellectual activity needed in executing it and the greater the amount of practice needed in order to master it. In playing music sensory feedback must be processed, sequences need to be remembered, and various musical and technical aspects require analysis.

Mental practice, as discussed in chapter II, inherently reinforces all these cognitive elements. Additional strategies for strengthening cognitive aspects include exercising mental leadership, developing verbal cues, and using physical models. These strategies will be discussed below.

• *Mental Leadership*

Mental practice has two basic functions: it heightens awareness of sensory feedback, and it allows the mind to be in conscious control, *directing* physical actions rather than just responding to them.

While playing, such mental leadership helps to maintain musical and technical continuity. To work on leading mentally, play at a tempo that allows you to continually imagine each sound, and the accompanying sensations of playing, a split-second before it actually happens.

The following exercise illustrates this principle: play a slow scale and during the last eighth-note value of each whole-note imagine playing the next pitch (fig. IV-1). Repeat the scale several times and gradually increase the tempo, staying mentally ahead of your body throughout. Then try the exercise with an actual piece of music.

With practice, mental leadership can become a healthy habit that keeps you physically prepared for meeting musical and technical demands as they arise. (Note: mental leadership is also important in sight-reading because the eyes need to be looking ahead, grouping notes into patterns and recognizing musical relationships.)

Fig. IV-1: Mental Leadership

play   (imagine) play   (imagine) play   (imagine) play

• *Verbal Cueing*

Verbal cueing is a strategy that both encourages thinking ahead and reinforces sequencing of events. Think of an occasion where you were playing your instrument while someone else—perhaps your teacher or a conductor—was calling out brief directions just before they wanted you to carry them out. The following exercise serves the same purpose, only in this case you are responsible for both jobs: for being the leader and the player simultaneously.

Choose a section of music that is fairly new to you or that has sequences that are hard to remember. Play the passage slowly, simultaneously describing essential aspects of your playing or of the music (either speak out loud or silently think your words). Once the most important aspects are clear to you, find a word or phrase to represent each point. Either write these verbal cues into the music or memorize them in their correct sequence. Repeat the passage at increasingly fast tempos, cueing each motion or musical nuance a moment before it should occur.

Fig. IV-2: Verbal Cues

The process of developing verbal cues is analogous to the process of learning a new recipe. At first all of the detailed cooking instructions need to be read, but once you've cooked that particular dish a few times, the various steps can be summarized in a few words: "boil, peel, mash while hot, add spices..." *The cues help ensure that each step occurs on time and in the right order.*

• *"Modeling"*

So-called "modeling" is a fundamental element in learning a physical skill. Essentially one watches or listens to a "model" and then copies the demonstrated skill. In a musical context, models include demonstrations and performances (live or recorded). Such models can be helpful during all stages of learning.

When something new is being learned, a model generally offers more information than can be absorbed at once. Therefore, one needs to first identify key technical and musical elements on which to focus. (Teachers can help their students to get the most out of demonstrations by directing their attention to specific points.) As new materials become more familiar, one's awareness can expand to include more detailed and subtle information.

When watching/listening to a model, you will benefit the most from actively *empathizing* with the player, rather than passively taking in the performance. For example, if you watch and empathize with a musician who has a particularly fluent technique, you may gain insight into how such playing might feel. By imagining the sensations being experienced by the performer, you form a mental model that can shape your own playing.

A model can also provide "prompting" that supports a mental rehearsal. For example, when memorizing a piece of music, you might listen to a recording of the piece while imagining the concurrent motions of playing. Since the recording provides the aural component, you can focus entirely on projecting the kinesthetic sensations. On the other hand, if you know the piece extremely well, a fun challenge might be to mentally stay a split-second *ahead* of the model, continuously anticipating both the sounds and the sensations of playing.

Category 2:
Mental Practice During
Different Stages Of Learning

Mental practice can be effectively used during all stages of learning. When something new is being learned, the focus of physical and mental rehearsals tends to be very detailed and specific. You are working to heighten sensory awareness and are analyzing technical and musical elements. As learning progresses, individual components become linked into cohesive sequences and you begin to focus more on the overall flow of playing.

This shift in focus can be supported through appropriate mental work. One very useful strategy is that of "practicing in units" (fig. IV-3). This exercise requires you to think ahead and to quickly grasp units of musical information. It also trains your body to remain relaxed and responsive to mental directives. All these aspects support the eventual projection of the overall musical flow.

To familiarize yourself with this practice strategy, choose a passage of music that consists primarily of running eighth or sixteenth notes. Instead of playing the music as written, group the notes into pairs, into triplets, or into units of four notes. Play each grouping quickly and follow it with a momentary pause. When this becomes comfortable, link these small units into longer sequences; play two or three (or more) groups in sequence before each pause. Then try pausing between each phrase or musical sequence.

During each pause think ahead and *imagine playing the next grouping of notes*. Mentally hear and feel each unit, vividly and accurately, *before* physically playing it. If needed, do *several* mental repetitions before going on to play. Also during each pause release any tension that might be present.

This exercise provides invaluable practice in anticipatory thinking, while also training your body to remain relaxed. Remember that when you play your piece *as written*, you can still think in terms of "units" to help your mind to stay ahead of your body.

Fig. IV-3: "Practicing in Units"

As written:

Practice:

play   play   play   play

(project)   (recall/project)   (recall/project)   (recall/project)   (recall)

Link Units:

(project)   play   (recall/project)   play   (recall)

Category 3:
Physiological Aspects
Of Mental Practice

What are the underlying mechanisms that allow mental practice to be so effective? How do mind and muscles interface in creating the measurable effects documented by researchers?

The brain with its two hemispheres is analogous to a command center with two contrasting but complementary areas of expertise. For example, the right hemisphere generally processes information pertaining to body image, the flow of movement sequences, and spatial relationships. The left hemisphere is more adept at linear thinking, analysis, and translating the mental images and representations of the right brain into words.

The right brain is responsible for influencing the form and quality of all our intentional movements. Whenever one decides to act physically, a momentary representation of the intended movement flashes through one's mind, triggering the appropriate muscular responses. Thought and movement are so closely linked that the two seem virtually simultaneous.

In fact though, the mental representation functions as a sort of "schema" or "blueprint" that allows the brain to organize and send appropriate signals to the muscles, via the "CNS"—the Central Nervous System. The CNS consists of brain and spinal cord. The "blueprint" for movement involves the motor cortex of the brain. Here, the necessary nerve-and-muscle units are selected and sequenced, ultimately creating coordinated movement.

Certain nerves branch out from the spinal cord to become "peripheral nerves" that contain a mix of motor and sensory fibers. The motor fibers relay the movement from the brain to the selected muscle groups, which then contract and/or relax in a coordinated sequence. The sensory fibers in the peripheral nerves provide immediate feedback about the movement. This is sent back up through the nerves and spinal cord for interpretation by the brain.

Based on this feedback, a new message is sent out via the motor fibers, containing directions for an appropriate response. The sensory fibers again provide feedback about a variety of sensory stimuli such as touch, position, pain, etc., that results in another modification, and so on. This ongoing interchange occurs with lightning speed and is generally referred to as a "feedback loop" (fig. IV-4). It is the mechanism by which one learns and refines a skill.

Fig. IV-4: Feedback Loop

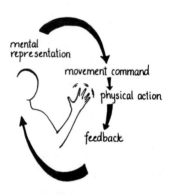

mental representation

movement command

physical action

feedback

• *Alternating Mental And Physical Rehearsals Creates A Feedback Loop*

Mental representations precede intentional motions. Conscious manipulation of these representations directly influences the movements that follow. For example, by imagining in vivid and accurate detail an action that lies within one's capacity, and by emphasizing qualities of efficiency and coordination in the imagined action, these desirable qualities will to some degree be embodied in the subsequent physical action. In turn, the improved quality of the action provides sensory feedback that can be used in refining the next mental rehearsal. In essence, here is another feedback loop, where the conscious refinement of mental representations directly influences physical performance, which helps improve the next mental representation, and so on.

• *Mental Rehearsals Cause Slight Muscular Contractions*

As discussed in Chapter II, mental representations must be clear and precise to be effective. Researchers have found that when movements are imagined very vividly, slight physical reactions are triggered in the body. The tiny responses occur in the *same* muscles and nerves that would be used during *physical* performance of the imagined movement. The responses are so minimal that EMG electrodes must be used in measuring the nerve and muscle activity.

While such tiny muscle contractions definitely accompany mental practice and may even send signals back to the brain, via the sensory fibers in the peripheral nerves, they don't seem to strengthen or adjust our mental representations. Some researchers argue otherwise, but the bulk of research indicates that the slight muscle responses do not account for mental practice effects. Instead, they may be an indicator of the *intensity* with which a person is imagining an action. Some researchers hypothesize that in experimental settings the quality of a person's mental practice may be monitored through ongoing measurement of muscular responses.[7] This possibility needs further investigation.

Category 4:
Effects Of Mental
Pre-Performance Strategies

• *Mental Rehearsal Just*
Prior To Performance

Some researchers have investigated the use of mental rehearsal just prior to performance of a skill. In their studies the subjects used brief mental rehearsals of the immediate task (rather than imagining actions that might happen later on in the performance). The results showed that in addition to preparing the nerves and muscles for action, the mental rehearsals promoted concentration and helped many performers to maintain a sense of confidence.

Therefore, just prior to playing, project your ideal mental model of the opening measures of music. In the course of playing a piece, mentally prepare entrances that follow rests. By engaging in such mental activity your mind remains focused on the task at hand, thereby reducing distracting thoughts. Furthermore, the knowledge that you are mentally in command may generate some extra self-assurance.

• *Creative Imagery For Performance Enhancement*

Another strategy that researchers have looked at is the use of creative imagery. There certainly is plenty of anecdotal evidence that creative imaginings can be helpful. However, the subjective component creates problems in experimental settings because it is difficult to quantify and to control for.

One study in particular clearly shows that the power of creative imagery depends on personal associations.[8] Working with a group of elite ice-skaters, the researchers described a specific image geared towards creating warmth, energy, and a peaceful attitude. This image was followed by a description of a perfect skating program. When asked about their inner experience, the response of the skaters was surprising. Each response was vastly different, ranging from very desirable to very destructive imaginings.

The overall conclusion was that, although the creative image was beneficial for some individuals, the same image could also be interpreted as symbolizing something negative. This is true of any image. Thus the creative imagery suggestions given in this book should be thought of as points of departure only—as ideas that are intended to stimulate creativity and to encourage personal exploration.

• *Developing Creative Images*

Creative images can be used along with mental rehearsals to establish a positive mind-set, to evoke the mood of the music, and to help create a sense of ease and strength in the body. Such images are helpful both during practice sessions and in performance settings. One relatively universal image is that of light (white or golden light is most common). This image is found in many meditation practices and is used symbolically in religious and poetic settings the world over.

When pictured in various forms, the image of light may be used to support several physical and mental aspects of playing and performance. For example, to counteract tension and to encourage a feeling of comfort while playing, try imagining something like a sun nestled in the center of your pelvis, sending waves of warmth and energy through your limbs.

To help you concentrate, imagine being surrounded by a bubble or barrier of light that shields you from distractions and from any perceived disapproval. If the emphasis is on communicating through music, imagine light connecting you with the audience and establishing rapport. And finally, if you tend to think of inspiration as coming from a source outside of yourself, use the image of light to symbolize a higher realm or creative source.

• *Rehearsing Creative Images*

The preceding imagery example deals with physical aspects of playing and performing. Of course you may also have images that help in summoning the mood of the music. (See chapter V for suggestions on using imagery for musical inspiration.)

How and when you conjure up various images is a matter of personal preference and experience. However, don't wait until an actual performance to start using images. Instead, develop effective strategies during practice sessions and then program yourself to recall specific images under pressure.

For example, rehearse the opening moments of a performance, including all mental preparations. Practice walking on and then tuning your instrument while scanning your body for balanced posture. During these preparations you can already bring up images that support your comfort on stage and that might help you to connect with the music. Then imagine playing the opening phrase(s) without any sense of hurry. Finally, begin playing physically.

With enough practice your mental preparations onstage will not take very long. However when going through your mental routine in practice sessions, imagine the audience waiting patiently. You certainly don't want to become so unexpectedly self-conscious when people are watching that you lose focus or rush through the preparations.

• *Make A Cue Card*

To help in rehearsing mental pre-performance sequences, try making a "cue card." Think of words or simple pictures that symbolize each step of the performance preparations. Then put these, in order, on a small card and post it on your stand. A sample sequence might be:

CENTER, BREATHE, CONNECT, MUSIC

The verbal cues in this example represent the following information:

1) CENTER: balance your posture, soften in all joints, and focus on feeling a sense of calm in your center of gravity (for most people this is located several inches below the navel, and slightly in front of the spine);

2) BREATHE: breathe in energy, breathe out tension, and rest more fully into your center;

3) CONNECT: form a connection with the audience;

4) MUSIC: focus on the opening phrases of the music, hearing the sounds in your mind to the exclusion of all else.

At first each step of preparation may need to be practiced individually and may take a fair amount of time to establish. However, with practice you will be able to call forth the desired mental and physical state quite quickly. After you reach this point, take advantage of every playing opportunity to practice the pre-performance sequence (during lessons, when playing for friends or family, in performance classes, at dress-rehearsals, etc.).

Shortly after each performance, go through a mental replay of the experience. Make a few notes on how effective the mental sequence was. In addition summarize the performance—note best moments, mistakes, changes in energy and emotions, level of concentration, etc. Analyze this information and use it in preparing for future performances. Keeping such a performance journal helps in tracking progress.

Summary

Research shows that mental practice positively influences the execution of fine motor skills such as the ones required in playing a musical instrument. Mental practice reinforces the cognitive aspects of musical learning by heightening physical aware-ness, strengthening sequential memory, and training analytical skills. Additional strategies to facilitate learning include exercises in mental leadership, verbal cueing, and modeling.

Mental practice is useful during all stages of learning. It supports the process of linking musical and technical components into cohesive sequences. It also helps to create and refine mental blueprints for action. These mental plans interface with the body via a complex feedback loop involving the central nervous system.

In addition to its daily applications, mental practice can be used just prior to performance. This increases muscular responsiveness and enhances concentration and confidence. Creative imagery provides another positive way to influence playing and may be effectively combined with realistic mental representations.

Both creative and realistic representations can be used in "pre-performance sequences" that are geared towards establishing an appropriate mind-set. Such sequences can be rehearsed long before they are used for performance.

CHAPTER V

FURTHER MENTAL PRACTICE STRATEGIES

Thus far in this book, mental practice has been defined and a basic training program has been outlined. Basic strategies for using mental practice and imagery have been presented as well. This chapter contains further strategies, some of which expand on previously discussed techniques. A more in-depth discussion of creative imagery is to be found here as well.

Perspective

When practicing mentally, either an internal or an external perspective may be used. With an internal perspective, the sights, sounds, and feelings of playing are imagined just as they are perceived—

from within the body. In contrast, an external perspective uses the viewpoint of an outsider who is watching one's playing.

• *The Internal Perspective Is Most Important*

When individuals begin to learn a complex skill, they often take an external perspective in imagining the skill. This parallels the information they have absorbed in *watching* a model. In addition, the external viewpoint probably reflects the individual's lack of sensory experience with the skill.

In contrast, skilled performers generally adopt the internal perspective,[9] emphasizing aural and kinesthetic sensations rather than visual feedback. Regardless of your skill level, you should make a conscious effort to take on the internal perspective right from the start because it directly reinforces the experience of playing and facilitates learning.

• *The Role Of An External Perspective*

Inner kinesthetic awareness is essential in achieving an efficient instrumental technique and is appropriate for virtually all mental rehearsals. However, the external viewpoint may be beneficial during performance preparations. So much time is spent in perfecting musical matters that the impact of stage presence on overall performance often is overlooked.

When someone projects poise and confidence, the audience generally feels more comfortable and enjoys the music more than when the performer appears insecure or distressed. Acting in a confident manner, regardless of one's actual feelings, can raise self-esteem by its proverbial bootstraps. On the other hand, one may unintentionally undermine a positive attitude through incongruous body language. The person who displays poor posture (i.e. slouching) may come across as insecure or apologetic, even when actually feeling positive and enthusiastic.

To address these concerns, mental preparations for performance might include visualizing deportment in walking onstage, the manner in which the audience is acknowledged, and overall body language while playing. Body movements that are in accord with musical content can add visually to a performance. Distracting mannerisms need to be eliminated.

These "externally viewed" aspects of performance also need rehearsal from the internal perspective. Using *both* viewpoints and combining these mental rehearsals with real-life practice in front of a mirror or video camera can make an appreciable difference.

Manipulating The Tempo Of Mental Rehearsals

Mental rehearsals usually are done in "real time," meaning both physical and mental performances are executed at the same rate of speed. However, occasional manipulation of the *mental* playing speed can be beneficial.

• *Mentally Playing In Slow Motion*

Slowing down mental representations creates the drawn-out effect of a slow-motion film. This can help in identifying movements and sensations that otherwise fly by unnoticed. Slowing down is especially useful in the beginning stages of learning a skill. The slower tempo helps to enrich one's sensory impressions, making them fuller and more complete. It also allows fuller exploration of motions that must be performed at a particular speed in order to maintain their technical integrity.

For example, a string player's spiccato or ricochet bowings depend largely on speed and momentum. Physically playing at a slower tempo would actually change the bowing technique, requiring a different use of the bow-hand to control the bow's bounce. However, a slow *mental* rehearsal would help the player to analyze the technique without unwanted physical changes.

For example, slow mental rehearsals might reveal that the free bounce of the bow is being inhibited by tension in the bow-hand. Further slow rehearsals would be used to analyze the source(s) of tension and to imagine playing in a more efficient manner. The subsequent physical rehearsals at the proper, faster tempo would be influenced by the awareness gained during slow mental rehearsals.

• *Mentally Projecting An Ideal Tempo*

If you cannot yet play a piece at its proper tempo, mental rehearsals of the final tempo help reinforce musical ideals. Decisions concerning technique often depend on tempo, as do details of interpretation. Thus the projected final tempo needs to guide your practice.

Keep in mind that incomplete and faulty repetitions inevitably attend any learning process. Regular projection of an ideal mental model helps reduce the amount of time spent playing erroneously; each physical repetition can be directed towards achieving the ideal. Naturally this ideal model will become fine-tuned as mental rehearsals and physical rehearsals are alternated.

• *Using A Mental "Fast Forward" Mode*

Another strategy for manipulating tempo is to move into a "fast-forward" mode. In this case, you mentally skim through the music to review specific spots that need attention. This is analogous to speed-reading when you already know the material, but are looking for specific points. Upon finding them, you slow down, make a mental note, and then resume skimming.

Similarly, when mentally speeding through some music, slow the tempo down on reaching the desired passages. Rehearse these spots as you come to them, or complete the review before going back to practice specific aspects. Such quick reviews can be done with or without printed music in hand.

A variation on the fast-forward review is to recall key entrances or other musical aspects, *in their correct sequence*, without reviewing the materials in between. Touch on these spots quickly and in succession to strengthen your memory of how they fit into the entire composition. If your emphasis isn't on sequencing, take time out to practice each spot, mentally and/or physically, using a normal tempo.

Miming As A Supplement To Mental And Physical Practice

The use of miming to reinforce mental work has been examined by researchers. In one study[10] four different practice strategies were compared, using college trombone players: 1) physical practice only; 2) mental practice only; 3) mental practice *while* miming; 4) combined physical and mental practice.

As expected the group using the combined mental and physical practice improved the most. Those practicing only physically were rated second in terms of improvement. In third place was the group using a combination of mental practice and miming (but with no physical practice on the instrument). This group improved *significantly more* than those players who practiced only mentally.

Such results indicate that miming, when used *while* rehearsing mentally, can actually heighten the effects of the mental work.[11] Perhaps miming is so helpful because it can prompt inner hearing. Often, one can more easily imagine the sounds of playing when supporting the mental representations with actual playing motions.

In addition, the miming motions provide kinesthetic feedback that can be analyzed and assimilated, without also having to process the aural feedback accompanying actual playing. This means you can focus exclusively on the sensations of each movement, on releasing any tension, and on exploring movements that might be more efficient than habitual ones.

Eliminating Negative Mental Representations

Mental representations greatly influence our learning and performance, so we need to eliminate (or transform) representations that might be detrimental to our actual physical playing. You can probably empathize with the scenario of performing a difficult piece and thinking, "Oh-oh, here comes the part that I never get right...careful now, watch out..."

And bang, you make a mistake. Either you miss something prior to the problem spot because of faltering concentration, or the dreaded mistake happens because you are focusing on the numerous times that the spot has been incorrectly played.

Negative mental representations program you to perform accordingly. When imagining something going awry, a faulty mental blueprint is created which competes with the correct aspects of your training. Furthermore, concentration is disturbed and confidence is undermined.

75

• *Research Findings*

Researchers have investigated the disturbing results of negative mental representations. Several studies have compared the effects of *negative* versus *successful* representations of performance. (Negative projections depict poorly executed skill sequences and/or blatant mistakes. Successful representations generally involve an ideal mental model.) The studies all show that faulty representations *significantly degrade* the subsequent physical performance of the particular skill in question.[12]

• *Imagining Outcome Versus Components*

One study in particular has shown that during performance, imagining the *outcome* of a skill sequence has greater beneficial effects than imagining the *individual movements* that make up the task.[13] In a musical context, this means that once you master a piece, the mental focus should be on projecting the overall flow of the music (the "outcome"). Of course you can still work on specific aspects of playing during practice sessions. However, when performing, the ideal focus is on how you *want* to sound and play, rather than on remembering various technical details.

• *A Strategy For Stopping*
Negative Representations

The first step in reducing negative representations while playing is to work on mentally playing through the music, reinforcing any weak representations until the mental performance goes without a hitch. You gain such mental control through the alternation of physical and mental rehearsals. This heightens sensory awareness and strengthens memory. If specific passages or musical sections are worked on, they also need to be practiced in context to establish the overall musical flow.

As the mental version of a piece becomes dependable, you can focus on dealing with negative thoughts that arise while playing. "Thought stopping" is a simple technique that is often taught by psycho-therapists and sports psychologists to help their clients shift mental focus. Basically the negative thought sequence is decisively interrupted using a verbal command, which can be accompanied by a particular image. This is followed by a conscious shift in emphasis. A positive mental representation, a positive affirmation, or other appropriate thought is chosen to replace the earlier, negative one.

For example, while playing you might be dwelling on a mistake that happened earlier. You could say (or think) "stop!" and let the image of a red stop sign flash through your mind. *Immediately* thereafter, you would refocus on maintaining mental leadership while continuing to play.

Experiment with different words and images to find something simple yet effective. Use the technique during practice sessions and try stopping negative thoughts in daily life situations as well. This way you will have experience with redirecting thoughts and will likely be able to do so even under pressure.

Fig. V-I: Stopping Negative Thoughts

• *Stopping Thoughts Is Not Always Appropriate*

One cautionary note concerning thought stoppage. Sometimes trying to stop or divert thoughts only makes their negative aspects seem stronger. Perhaps your negative perceptions warrant consideration, although they are disruptive at the present moment. Try imagining that the thoughts have been written on a piece of paper and put into a box for safekeeping. Promise yourself that you will come back to them at a more appropriate time (and be sure to follow through). Another possibility is to immerse yourself into the negative perceptions temporarily, perhaps even exaggerating them and imagining how much worse things *could* be than they *actually* are. Then assume a more objective viewpoint. Consider the larger context of the situation and try to put the negative thoughts into their proper perspective.

Finally, instead of manipulating your thoughts at all you might simply take note of them with an attitude of acceptance and move on. Again sometimes less is more.

Imagery For Musical And Technical Inspiration

Most mental practice techniques rely on realistic mental representations where sensory awareness and accurate mental models are quintessential factors. Creative images that symbolize particular qualities can add a complementary and inspiring element to the "realistic" work. Chapter III (on mental training) touched upon the use of creative imagery to support movement. Chapter IV presented some ideas for using creative imagery in performance situations. Below are suggestions that pertain more to daily musical work.

• *Take Advantage Of Spontaneous Images*

Creative images that somehow relate to musical interpretation or to technical aspects of playing often pop into mind spontaneously. A string player working on slow, sustained bow strokes may think of moving through thick molasses. Or a flutist might be practicing a very fast passage and suddenly be struck by the image of nimble clowns dancing across the keys.

Rather than letting such thoughts flit through your mind only to disappear, you can retain the images to inspire specific attributes while playing. Calling up images that symbolize particular qualities can often be as effective, if not more so, than concentrating only on the physical aspects of producing music.

Try keeping a notebook of images that occur to you. Record the image and the musical or technical quality that it parallels. Then see if the same image is useful in different contexts. Returning to the bowing example above, you might write: "*moving through molasses*: comfortable resistance, sustained sense of pulling horizontally; came up during slow bowing in scales." Then you would try applying the image in other passages requiring sustained bowing.

• *Coming Up With Images*
When images don't occur on their own, try jump-starting your creativity by using *words*. For example, in looking for an image to support a certain physical sensation, try saying out-loud, *"I feel like...,"* or *"I am..."* and see if an image comes up to help you complete the sentence.

For sensations in specific body parts, begin with *"My arm feels...,"* *"My fingers are...,"* etc. When working on a particular musical quality, start sentences with *"This sounds like..."* or *"I hear a...."* And so on.

To illustrate: *"I feel like...I'm playing under water"* might describe a buoyant, fluid sensation. Or, *"I am...steady as a rock"* might come to mind when keeping a constant tempo. When using this verbal strategy, keep your mind quiet and take the first thought that comes, rather than *trying* to think of a good image.

Even after forming effective images, try verbalizing them as they come up during practice sessions. For instance, to bring an expansive calm to a particular musical passage, you could say, *"I feel like a king (or queen)"* <u>before</u> you rehearse that section. This may bring greater clarity and emphasis to your intentions.

• *Images Can Change*

No matter how wild or whimsical an image is, it can be used to your advantage if it somehow captures a quality you are looking for. Don't count on the same image working all the time, however. Sometimes images seem to lose their "charge" after a while and new ones are needed. When images lose their effectiveness, possibly your perspective on the music or movement has changed. Then a new image is needed simply because you are now looking for a different quality.

• *Sharing Your Images With Others*

When working with other musicians, we often need to share our personal perceptions of the music and of how it might be played. In addition to describing the actions and physical sensations of playing, we need to communicate about the less tangible aspects of music. This can be effectively accomplished by using evocative words and colorful phrases to fuel the musical imagination of students and colleagues.

By describing music through poetic images, you can shape the way others play that same music. Fellow musicians empathize with the sounds and sensations being conveyed by the images and then translate these into physical playing. If the ensuing sound is not what you intended, find a different image, or bridge the gap between image and music with more concrete, technical directions.

For example, if a violin student doesn't understand what is meant by a "glassy and transparent" sound, a demonstration of the sound may bring about the response, "Oh, I hear what you mean." Further instructions on controlling the bow and fingers may still be necessary before the student can manage to produce that "glassy" sound, but a balance has been struck between musical inspiration (through imagery) and technical execution.

Summary

This chapter has presented a number of ways to manipulate mental representations and to use imagery.

Perspective: When practicing mentally, the internal perspective should be used almost exclusively because it parallels the actual experience of playing. However an external perspective may be useful when rehearsing stage presence. You can watch an ideal "mental movie" of yourself, manipulating it to reflect qualities you strive for in real life.

Tempo can be manipulated while rehearsing mentally. Rehearsing at a pace slower than your physical playing may bring greater clarity and accuracy to the mental representations. This is helpful when learning something new, when working on problem spots, and when an action can't physically be slowed down without essentially changing its technical aspects.

When unable to physically carry out a skill at its proper tempo, mental rehearsals can shift between reproducing the current physical tempo and projecting the final, faster speed.

A third manipulation involves a "fast forward" mode for skimming through the music to find specific areas that need work. This involves a quick review of entrance sequences, specific passages, and musical sections, skipping the materials in between.

Miming is useful both for supporting inner hearing and for refining physical playing motions. When simulating playing, you can focus exclusively on kinesthetic feedback, on releasing muscular tension, and on attaining a free and easy flow of movement, without feeling restricted by the demands of the instrument. Once these sensations are accessed and practiced, they should transfer easily to actual playing.

Negative mental representations are detrimental because they provide a faulty blueprint for action, plus they interrupt concentration and undermine confidence. The first step is to develop a strong mental representation of excellent playing. Then, if negative thoughts intrude, you can: 1) interrupt and redirect them, 2) "save" the thoughts for later, 3) delve fully into the thoughts to come up with a more objective assessment, or 4) simply accept the negative as part of a larger context, without dwelling on it.

Creative images provide an important counterpart to purely technical discussions of music and its production. Images that embody a particular quality can actually support the brain's activity in organizing movement to produce desired musical or technical effects.

Images can be entirely spontaneous or somewhat planned, with particular images evoking certain physical qualities. Such images can be used to shape both your own playing and that of fellow musicians.

APPENDICES

• *Introduction to the Appendices*

The following appendices contain materials that cannot exactly be classified as mental practice strategies and yet have a direct bearing upon the materials presented in the main body of the book.

The section on teaching mental practice skills to young students is found here simply because it doesn't gracefully fit into the main chapters.

The topic of relaxation elaborates on certain suggestions contained in the previous chapters. Furthermore, many relaxation techniques depend on some form of imagery for effectiveness.

The subject of healing with imagery is included because so many musicians do experience some form of pain or injury at some point in their playing lives. As long as you have mental practice and imagery skills (which it is hoped will aid in *preventing* injury), why not apply these skills to situations outside of the practice room and the stage?

APPENDIX A:
Teaching Mental Practice Techniques to Young Students

Mental practice techniques can be scaled down to suit the needs and abilities of young students and beginners. Learning to play an instrument requires a progression of increasing challenges. Plant the seeds of mental practice and imagery skills early and foster them over time.

At each lesson, guide the student's awareness of specific physical sensations. Even very young children can be taught to distinguish between "soft, comfie" versus "tight, icky" sensations in the muscles. Then guide the student in using very basic mental practice skills (see below). In addition to giving directions, ask the student about his or her inner experience. You may find that what is actually being imagined is quite different from what you are asking for.

While a student may respond positively to mental training during lessons, don't assume that he or she will be able to manage without guidance at home. Write out short, specific mental practice and imagery exercises to make things more concrete. Also try enlisting parents to help with the child's mental rehearsals. For best results teach the parents right along with the child, at least initially. If parents have some first-hand experience of mental work, they will be far more effective in helping their child.

Beginning Mental Practice

Several times per lesson, have your student carry out a very short, simple action followed by a mental rehearsal of the action. First try big motions involving the whole body or an entire limb, then have the child mime playing motions. Point out specific kinesthetic sensations, and then ask the child to mentally recreate the particular action.

Work on ear-training in the same way. First play a note, melody, etc., and have the child sing it back. Then play the same thing again, and ask the student to repeat the sounds mentally.

While teaching, you might say, "Let's pretend that you're magical and can play your instrument just by thinking about it." "Can you hear this note in your head?" "Can you 'feel' this motion?" And so on. Keep alternating physical actions and mental recall. In time you can increase the frequency and complexity to include more of the strategies discussed throughout this book.

Creative Images

Children thrive on activities that speak to their imaginations. Be creative in using images to shape both their instrumental technique and their musical ear. Think of childlike stories and dramas that can be expressed through the music. Or do activities that foster attentive listening without the extra challenge of managing the instrument.

Improvise a simple piece with great variation in articulation, dynamic, tempo, etc. Characterize the variations imaginatively. For example:

> *staccatto* sounds like a jumping rabbit;
> *glissando* swoops like a bird;
> *pianissimo* is like tiptoeing around a
> sleeping baby;

Then, have the student move to the music, acting out its character. Be prepared to do a lot of prompting at first. You are training listening skills as well as dealing with possible self-consciousness. You will be more successful at engaging the child if you model possible motions, or if you sing the music and act it out alongside the child.

Take Breaks

The habit of taking constructive breaks can be taught from day one. Singing and ear training, easy stretches and fun physical activities are all options for preventing mental and physical boredom or fatigue. More quiet activities like age-appropriate affirmations and visualizations are further options for shaping breaks. (See *To Learn With Love*, by W. and C. Starr, for other ideas.) Be sure to enrich each activity with some sort of imaginative component, and above all, have fun!

APPENDIX B:
Relaxation

Conscious relaxation is fundamental in developing a healthy instrumental technique and in preventing injury. Fortunately, the ability to relax at will is a skill that can be trained like any other. Regular practice at entering a state of deep relaxation helps develop a secure memory of the sensations associated with being tension-free.

• The Relaxation Response

Researchers have found that spending 15-20 minutes in a state of deep relaxation unburdens the nervous system and allows the body to re-establish its equilibrium.[14] Deep relaxation creates a number of beneficial effects, including a reduction in blood pressure, a slowing of metabolic activity, decreased tension in deep skeletal muscles that are generally beyond conscious control, and the formation of brain-waves that are remarkably regular and synchronized (in contrast to those found during waking, sleeping, and dreaming).[16]

This group of bodily reactions is sometimes called "the relaxation response." The physiological state is exactly the opposite of that experienced under stress. Numerous studies show that when deep relaxation is practiced regularly (ideally twice a day), the cumulative effect may be the *reversal* of many stress-induced symptoms.[16]

• *Deep Relaxation Techniques*

Three techniques that are commonly used to bring about a state of deep relaxation are: meditation, autogenic training, and biofeedback therapy. These three techniques all use some form of imagery to calm the mind and call forth the relaxation response.

Meditation involves focusing on a single word, sound, thought, or image for an extended period of time. If other thoughts intrude, they are gently disregarded in a passive, relaxed style.

Autogenic training is a specific sequence of verbal suggestions that direct certain physical sensations. Mental representations or images accompany the suggestions to promote the specific feelings. The combination of words and images is directed at creating warmth and heaviness in the arms and legs, a calm and steady heartbeat, a cool forehead, and a warm abdominal area. All of these sensations are linked to the relaxation response.

Biofeedback therapy uses imagery and verbal affirmations to influence physical functions. Machines that detect subtle physical changes monitor the physical responses to these mental activities. Thoughts or representations that consistently trigger the same physical reaction can be identified. If the correlation is desirable, the mind-body connection can be intensified through repetition. When certain mental activity calls forth negative responses, conscious effort can be made to replace the negative activity with more desirable thoughts, images, and representations.

• *Examples Of Other Relaxation Techniques*

Relaxation techniques generally fall into two categories:

1) Those working "from the inside out" emphasize the creation of a peaceful mental state, allowing the body to relax. The three techniques discussed above all exemplify this approach.

2) Those working "from the outside in" focus on the release of physical tension, which in turn facilitates mental and emotional relaxation. Below are some examples.

Yoga stretches, deep breathing exercises, and "progressive muscle relaxation" (alternately tensing and then relaxing individual muscle groups throughout the body) all help to release physical tension. When appropriate imagery is used during such exercises, additional release may be achieved.

For instance, while stretching you might visualize all the targeted muscles softening and lengthening. While breathing deeply (specific breathing exercises are often a part of yoga training), you might imagine that the entire body is responding to the breathing motions. If you are doing a progressive muscle relaxation, you might imagine increased warmth and blood flow in the muscles as they relax.

Sometimes, stress can be most effectively released through vigorous physical activity rather than through a quiet relaxation exercise. Even then you can use visualization to support the release of pent-up tension. For example, while running or dancing you might focus on the sensations of breathing and imagine that each inhalation draws in nourishing energy and that each exhalation dispels stress.

• *Guided Visualizations Can Help Clear The Mind*

If you don't wish to practice relaxation techniques on a regular basis, guided visualizations may be useful for occasions when you *do* want to relax and clear the mind. A visualization such as the one given below can be especially useful before practicing mentally for an extended period of time.

Sample Visualization Script

Close your eyes and take a deep breath... exhale and let go of all the worries of the day... take a few more breaths, inhaling energy and nourishment and exhaling any tension... keep breathing slowly and deeply... feel your body relax completely... you feel so warm and heavy... continue breathing slowly, and now imagine that you are going down some deep, dark stairs... keep going down until you come to a door at the bottom... slowly open the door...

Step through the entrance and into a beautiful garden... it's full of flowers... there's a fountain nearby... go and sit near the fountain... you can smell the earth... listen to the gentle trickle of the water... you hear the birds singing... feel the warm sunshine on your body... there's a little breeze too, gently touching your skin...

Now think about your music... you can hear it... it's so beautiful... you love to play it... it comes so easily to you... you can feel yourself play...

(At this point, add any pertinent directions or affirmations, and leave sufficient time to practice mentally.)

Now, taking the sound of the music with you, walk back to the doorway at the edge of the garden... go slowly up the stairs... you are getting close to the top... on the last five stairs, count backwards from five to one, and as you count, you will be waking up, feeling refreshed and entirely aware of your surroundings...

"Five"... move your legs around a bit... "four"... move your arms a little... "three"... move your head around... "two"... you are waking up; take a deep breath... "one"... you are entirely awake and aware of your surroundings... take another deep breath... let your body stretch and move around... open your eyes and continue breathing slowly and deeply as you take in your surroundings...

If you have a hard time carrying out a visuali-zation just by thinking through it, have someone else read the script out-loud for you. Or, try making a tape-recording. Read in a gentle, soothing voice and leave about three seconds of silence between each image. In time you will be able to go through the visualization without the prompt of the tape.

If the visualization is practiced often enough, you may no longer need to go through the entire script to enter a state of relaxation. Simply thinking of "the garden" may be enough to bring up the peaceful feelings associated with it. If you get to this point, try using the image to center yourself just before practicing or performing a piece. Before calling up the image, though, consciously bring your body into a balanced and tension-free position.

• When Relaxed, Use Affirmations

When you are in a deeply relaxed state, your mind becomes very open to suggestion. This is a good time to support both self-image and musical work by using "affirmations." (Affirmations can be used for all manner of personal growth. Two excel-lent resources for this are *Creative Visualization* by S. Gawain, and *In The Mind's Eye*, by M. and N. Samuels.)

Affirmations are short, concise statements that describe your ideal self and your desired achieve-ments. They are stated in the present tense, as if the intended goals are already a reality. For example, say, *"I feel strong and I radiate confidence"* rather than saying, *"I would like to become strong and confident."* The second statement is tentative while the first is convincing, which is just the point. If you truly believe in yourself and are convinced of your abilities, you are more likely to actualize your ambitions than if you are pursued by self-doubt.

Affirmations are expressed positively, stating what you actually *want* rather than reiterating what you'd like to be rid of. For example, instead of thinking, *"I refuse to get tense while playing,"* find pro-active words to express the same intention: *"I am calm and centered...I play with fluid motions."* Along with affirmations for transforming negative tendencies, reinforce personal strong points and affirm those aspects that satisfy you.

Although affirmations are most effective when used in a relaxed state, they can be repeated frequently throughout the day, so that they become ingrained in your thinking. Write them down and post a copy of the list in any place that will catch your eye. Every time that you are reminded of the affirmations, take a deep breath and then exhale slowly while releasing as much tension as possible. Then dwell upon at least one affirmation before resuming your activities.

APPENDIX C:
Using Imagery To Support The Healing And Rehabilitation Of Injuries

• *Imagery Influences "Involuntary" Functions*

Mental imagery is a potent tool for influencing bodily functions normally considered beyond conscious control ("involuntary"). Working with advanced meditators, scientists have had a chance to study certain physical effects of mental control.

For example, quite a few Indian yogis have shown remarkable control over involuntary functions such as heartbeat and metabolic rate.[17] In another study, several Tibetan monks demonstrated incredible control over their body temperature.[18] Meditation, which inherently uses some form of imagery, was used in achieving these astonishing physical effects.

• *The Placebo Effect Stems From Mental Representations*

Medical researchers have learned that imagery can be used to support the functions of our immune system and to trigger the body's self-healing mechanisms.[19]

These findings are dramatically illustrated by the so-called placebo effect, where a person's mental activity causes a significant physical change in body chemistry and sensation, even in the absence of any medical intervention. In other words, people who imagine that a particular remedy will help them to regain their health may well experience relief from their symptoms upon using the remedy, even if the ingredients are considered chemically inert.

This placebo effect is so prevalent that every pharmaceutical company utilizes a double-blind arrangement for its drug testing: neither the testers nor the subjects know who is receiving a "mock-up" of the drug and who is receiving the real thing. In any test there are a percentage of subjects whose condition improves notably, in spite of the fact that they received a sugar pill instead of an actual drug. For example, in a series of carefully controlled studies in pain reduction, the placebo was 56 percent as effective as a dose of morphine![20]

The successful use of imagery to support healing also has been documented. Even serious diseases like cancer may respond positively to intensive imagery programs.[21] Clearly, the images we maintain concerning our physical well-being can profoundly affect our health.

• *Imagery For The Injured Musician*

The use of imagery to support healing and rehabilitation is relevant to musicians because of the high incidence of work-related injuries in the field. In a study of overuse-syndrome in professional musicians, H.J.H. Fry reported that the incidence of injury was *in excess of 50%* in all orchestras studied.[22]

When injured, it's in your best interest to mobilize all resources, including your mental capacities, in order to speed recovery and a subsequent return to playing. While professional help in diagnosing and treating musical injuries is highly recommended, don't discount your own capacities for healing.

• *Effective Images*

To be effective, healing images need to be consonant with reality. If you have an injury, form as accurate and clear an idea of the problem as possible. Specific images can in fact result in corresponding physical changes, so your intentions need to be directed appropriately.

Start by studying an anatomy book, using the diagrams to help locate the pain more accurately and to determine which structures and tissues might be affected. When discussing your injury with health-care practitioners, ask them to explain fully the reasoning behind their recommendations and to point you towards relevant resources and reading materials.

• *Developing Images To Support Healing*

In developing healing images, focus on supporting the functions of your body and on enhancing the effects of treatment interventions. Also concentrate on a "final state" image of the injured area, as though it were fully healed. A series of images encompassing all these aspects is probably most effective. You can combine realistic, physiological images with more symbolic representations. (See *Imagery In Healing* by Jeanne Achterberg for a thoroughly researched exploration of imagery in healing.)

For example, begin a succession of healing images for tendinitis with an overall image of the injured area, its joint(s), ligaments, tendons, and muscles. Follow this with a vision of cool white light bathing the area, reducing any swelling and washing away possible scar tissue. Imagine the healing process of the tendon tissues, likening the collagen strands that rebuild tendons to miniscule spaghetti strands.[23] Then envision the strands as neatly aligned in the direction of the tendon units rather than as a disorganized jumble. In the final image, depict yourself playing music with vigor and enjoyment, altogether free of pain.

• *Use Imagery To Support Rehabilitation*

As healing progresses and rehabilitation begins, use imagery to support any therapeutic modalities being employed. Continuing with the tendinitis example: two therapies that are commonly used in treating tendinitis are resistance exercises for strengthening the regenerating tissues and massage for stretching and relaxing them.

Check your anatomy book before doing strengthening exercises and then support the movements through realistic and creative images. Rather than focusing on the sensations of moving against resistance, imagine the movements happening with flowing ease (as they would if you were exercising in a deep pool of water). Monitor the rest of your body, making sure that it remains free of tension. Then during massage or other forms of therapeutic tissue manipulation, imagine that the therapist's hands radiate warmth and healing energy. (Many other images are possible, of course. Experiment and find something that works for you.)

• *Think Of Imagery As "Mental Medicine"*

The intention of healing imagery is to actually mobilize the body's healing mechanisms. Meditate on your images regularly to maximize their effectiveness[24] (if possible, twice a day for 20 minutes each time). Think of the images as "mental medicine," to be taken on a prescribed schedule. Also, create numerous opportunities each day for rehearsing key images and affirmations. Healing can be a lengthy process, and your patience may be sorely tried, so include affirmations to generally support a positive attitude.

Closing Comments

This book has presented a broad range of mental practice techniques and creative imagery suggestions. Throughout, various research findings have been cited or highlighted. To read more about research studies in the area of mental practice and imagery, an excellent introductory source is Chapter 11 in *Advances In Sport Psychology*, edited by T. S. Horn. There you will find an overview that includes many of the latest findings. Over 200 cited studies and other sources can be used in pursuing your own angle of interest.

Training your own skills may not come easily, so remember to take things one step at a time. Reading about mental practice techniques can make them seem overly complicated. Don't worry. Just take a leap of faith, try out the suggestions with an open mind, and rediscover an ability that is *innate to everyone*.

Enjoy, and good luck on your journey!

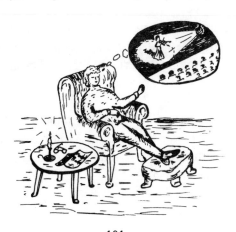

REFERENCES

[1] Samuel Applebaum, and Sada Applebaum. 1955. *With the Artists: World Famed String Players Discuss Their Art*. New York: John Markert and Co. 55.

[2] Frederick H. Martens. 1919. *Violin Mastery: Talks With Master Violinists and Teachers*. New York: Frederick A. Stokes, Co. 105.

[3] M. Denis. 1985. "Visual Imagery and the Use of Mental Practice in the Development of Motor Skills," *Canadian Journal of Sport Science* 10:8S-10S.

[4] Robert Weinberg. 1982. "The Relationship Between Mental Preparation Strategies and Motor Performance: A Review and Critique," *Quest* 33:200.

[5] Frederick Polnauer and Morton Marks. 1964. *Senso-Motor Study and Its Application to Violin Playing*. Illinois: American String Teachers Association 33.

[6] Deborah Feltz and Daniel Landers. 1983. "The Effects of Mental Practice on Motor Skill Learning and Performance: A Meta-Analysis," *Journal of Sport Psychology* 5:25-57.

[7] E. I. Bird and V. E. Wilson. 1988. "The Effects of Physical Practice Upon Psycho-physiological Response During Mental Rehearsal of Novice Conductors," *Journal of Mental Imagery* 12:62.

[8] S. M. Murphy and D. P. Jowdy. 1992. "Imagery and Mental Practice," in *Advances in Sport Psychology*, ed. by T. S. Horn. Champaign, Illinois: Human Kinetics Publishers 239.

[9] Dorothy Harris and William Robinson. 1986. "The Effects of Skill Level on EMG Activity During Internal and External Imagery," *Journal of Sport Psychology* 8:109.

[10] S. L. Ross. 1985. "The Effectiveness of Mental Practice in Improving the Performance of College Trombonists," *Journal of Research in Music Education* 33:221-230.

[11] Murphy and Jowdy 224-225.

[12] Robert Woolfolk, Shane Murphy, David Gottesfeld, and David Aitken. 1985. "Effects of Mental Rehearsal of Task Motor Activity and Mental Depiction of Task Outcome on Motor Skill Performance," *Journal of Sport Psychology* 7:196.

[13] Ibid. 196.

[14] Herbert Benson. 1975. *The Relaxation Response*. New York: Avon Books 5.

[15] Harold Bloomfield, Michael Cain and Dennis Jaffe. 1975. *TM: Discovering Inner Energy and Overcoming Stress*. New York: Delacorte Press 65.

[16] Ibid. 63-90.

[17] Ibid. 64.

[18] Benson 55.

[19] Jeanne Achterberg. 1985. *Imagery in Healing: Shamanism and Modern Medicine.* Boston: Shambhala Publications Inc. 175.

[20] Thomas Hanna. 1988. *Somatics: Reawakening the Mind's Control of Movement, Flexibility, and Health.* Reading, Massachusetts: Addison-Wesley Publishing Co. 86.

[21] Mike Samuels, M.D. and Nancy Samuels. 1975. *Seeing With the Mind's Eye: the History, Techniques, and Uses of Visualization.* New York: Random House Bookworks 226.

[22] Hunter J. H. Fry. June, 1986. "Incidence of Overuse Syndrome in the Symphony Orchestra," *Medical Problems of Performing Artists,* vol. 1. 2:55.

[23] John Jerome. June, 1985. "A Window of Healing: The Ultra-Specific Rehabilitation of Tendinitis," *Outside* 25.

[24] Achterberg 107.

BIBLIOGRAPHY

Achterberg, Jeanne. *Imagery in Healing: Shamanism and Modern Medicine*. Boston: Shambhala Publications Inc., 1985.

Andersen, Mark and Jean Williams. "A Model of Stress and Athletic Injury: Prediction and Prevention." *Journal of Sport and Exercise Psychology* 10 (1988): 294-306.

Andre, John, and John Means. "Rate of Imagery in Mental Practice: an Investigation." *Journal of Sport Psychology* 8 (1986): 124-128.

Anshel, Mark. "Applied Sport Psychology." In *Introduction to Applied Psychology*, ed. W.L. Gregory and W.J. Burroughs, 424-456. Illinois: Scott, Foresman, and Co. 1989.

Applebaum, Samuel, and Sada Applebaum. *With the Artists: World Famed String Players Discuss Their Art*. New York: John Markert and Co., 1955.

Auken, Richard Van, and Paul Larson. "Teaching Inner Hearing." *American Music Teacher* (April/May 1988).

Benson, Herbert. *The Relaxation Response*. New York: Avon Books, 1975.

Benson, Herbert. *Beyond the Relaxation Response.* New York: Berkley Publishing Group, 1984.

Bird, E. I., & Wilson, V. E. "The Effects of Physical Practice Upon Psycho-Physiological Response During Mental Rehearsal of Novice Conductors." *Journal of Mental Imagery* 12 (1988): 51-64.

Bloomfield, Harold, Michael Cain and Dennis Jaffe. *TM: Discovering Inner Energy and Overcoming Stress.* New York: Delacorte Press, 1975.

Denis, M. "Visual Imagery and the Use of Mental Practice in the Development of Motor Skills." *Canadian Journal of Sport Science* 10 (1985): 4S-16S.

Dorcas, Susan. *The Psychology of Sport—the Behavior, Motivation, Personality and Performance of Athletes.* New York: Van Nostrand Reinhold Co., 1987.

Feltz, Deborah. "Self-Confidence and Sports Performance.," In *Exercise and Sport Sciences Reviews*, ed. K.B. Pandolf, 16: 423-457. Baltimore: Williams and Wilkins, 1988.

Feltz, Deborah, and Daniel Landers. "The Effects of Mental Practice on Motor Skill Learning and Performance: A Meta-Analysis." *Journal of Sport Psychology* 5 (1983): 25-57.

Finke, Ronald. "Mental Imagery and the Visual System." *Scientific American*, (March 1986): 88-95.

Freymuth, Malva. "Response to Reader Query: Using Imagery to Facilitate Warm-Up." *Strings*, XI, no. 5 (January/February 1997), 24-25.

Freymuth, Malva. "Mental Practice: Some Guidelines for Musicians," *American Music Teacher*, 43, no. 5 (April/May 1994), 18-21.

Freymuth, Malva. "Mental Practice for Musicians: Theory and Application," *Medical Problems of Performing Artists*, 8, no. 4 (December 1993), 141-143.

Freymuth, Malva. *The Application of Sport Psychology Principles to Music Learning and Performance*. University of Colorado, unpublished D.M.A. thesis, 1991.

Freymuth, Malva. *Violin Playing From the Perspective of Mental Involvement and Physical Release*. University of Colorado, unpublished M.M. thesis, 1988.

Freymuth, Malva. *A Summary of Common Medical Problems of Musicians, Their Treatment, and Their Prevention*. University of Colorado, unpublished B.A. thesis, 1987.

Fry, Hunter J. H. "Incidence of Overuse Syndrome in the Symphony Orchestra." *Medical Problems of Performing Artists* 1, no. 2 (June 1986): 55.

Gawain, Shakti. *Creative Visualization*. New York: Bantam Books, 1978.

Gill, Diane. *Psychological Dynamics of Sport.* Champaign, Illinois: Human Kinetics Publishers, Inc., 1986.

Gray, J. J., & Haring, M. J. "Mental Rehearsal for Sport Performance: Exploring the Relaxation-Imagery Paradigm." *Journal of Sport Behavior* 7 (1984): 68-78.

Hale, Bruce. "The Effects of Internal and External Imagery on Muscular and Ocular Concomitants." *Journal of Sport Psychology* 4 (1982): 379-387.

Hall, Evelyn, and Elizabeth Erffmeyer. "The Effect of Visuo-Motor Behavior Rehearsal With Video-taped Modeling on Free Throw Accuracy of Inter-collegiate Female Basketball Players." *Journal of Sport Psycholog,* 5 (1983): 343-346.

Hall, Craig, and John Pongrac. *Movement Imagery Questionnaire.* Ontario, Canada: The University of Western Ontario, 1983.

Hanna, Thomas. *Somatics: Reawakening the Mind's Control of Movement, Flexibility, and Health.* Reading, Massachusetts: Addison-Wesley Publishing Co., 1988.

Harris, Dorothy. "Cognitive Skills and Strategies for Maximizing Performance." In *The Elite Athlete*, ed. N.K. Butts, T.T. Gushiken, and B. Zarins, 145-162. New York: Spectrum Publications, Inc., 1985.

Harris, Dorothy. "Relaxation and Energizing Techniques for Regulation of Arousal." In *Applied Sport Psychology: Personal Growth to Peak Performance*, ed. Jean Williams), 185-207. California: Mayfield Publishing Co., 1986.

Harris, Dorothy, and Bette Harris. *The Athlete's Guide to Sport Psychology: Mental Skills for Physical People*. Illinois: Leisure Press, 1984.

Harris, Dorothy, and William Robinson. "The Effects of Skill Level on EMG Activity During Internal and External Imagery." *Journal of Sport Psychology* 8 (1986): 105-111.

Hecker, J. E., & Kaczor, L. M. "Application of Imagery Theory to Sport Psychology: Some Preliminary Findings." *Journal of Sport and Exercise Psychology* 10 (1988): 363-373.

Jerome, John. "A Window of Healing: The Ultra-Specific Rehabilitation of Tendinitis." *Outside* (May 1985): 25-26.

Martens, Frederick H. *Violin Mastery: Talks With Master Violinists and Teachers*. New York: Frederick A. Stokes, Co., 1919.

Martens, Rainer. *Coaches Guide to Sport Psychology*. Illinois: Human Kinetics Publishers, 1987.

Masters, Robert, and Jean Houston. *Listening To the Body: the Psychophysical Way to Health and Awareness*. New York: Dell Publishing Co., 1978.

May, Jerry R. "Psychological Aspects of Athletic Performance: An Overview." In *The Elite Athlete*, ed. by N.K. Butts, T.T. Gushiken, and B. Zarins, 119-144. New York: Spectrum Publications, Inc., 1985.

McCullagh, Penny, Maureen Weiss, and Dianne Ross. "Modeling Considerations in Motor Skill Acquisition and Performance: An Integrated Approach." *Exercise and Sport Sciences Reviews*, ed. K.B. Pandolf, 17: 475-513. Baltimore: Williams and Wilkins, 1989.

Mumford, B., and C. Hall. "The Effects of Internal and External Imagery on Performing Figures in Figure Skating." *Canadian Journal of Sport Sciences*, 10 (1985): 171-177.

Murphy, S. M., and D. P. Jowdy. "Imagery and Mental Practice." In *Advances in Sport Psychology*, ed. T. S. Horn, 221-250. Champaign, Illinois: Human Kinetics Publisher, 1992.

Nideffer, Robert. *The Inner Athlete: Mind Plus Muscle for Winning*. New York: Thomas Y. Crowell Co., 1976.

Oxendine, J.B. "Emotional Arousal and Motor Performance." *Quest* 13 (1970): 23-32.

Paivio, A. "Cognitive and Motivational Functions of Imagery in Human Performance." *Canadian Journal of Sport Science* 10 (1985): 22S-28S.

Polnauer, Frederick, and Morton Marks. *Senso-Motor Study and Its Application to Violin Playing*. Illinois: American String Teachers Association, 1964.

Robbins, Anthony. *Unlimited Power*. New York: Ballantine Books, 1986.

Ryan, E. D. "Experimental Error in Psychological Research: a Reaction to 'Mental Practice and Knowledge of Results in the Learning of a Perceptual Motor Skill'." *Journal of Sport Psychology* 5 (1983): 108-110.

Sage, George. *Motor Learning and Control: A Neuropsychological Approach.* Dubuque, Iowa: Wm. C. Brown Publishers, 1984.

Samuels, Mike, and Nancy Samuels. *Seeing With the Mind's Eye: the History, Techniques, and Uses of Visualization.* New York: Random House Bookworks, 1975.

Starr, William and Constance. *To Learn With Love: a Companion for Suzuki Parents.* Knoxville, Tennessee: Kingston Ellis Press, 1983.

Sweigard, Lulu. *Human Movement Potential: Its Ideokinetic Facilitation.* Lanham, Maryland: Harper and Row Publishers, 1974.

Syer, John, and Christopher Connolly. *Sporting Mind, Sporting Body: An Athlete's Guide to Mental Training.* New Jersey: Prentice Hall, 1984.

Vealey, R. S. "Imagery Training for Performance Enhancement." In *Applied Sport Psychology: Personal Growth to Peak Performance*, ed. J. M. Williams, 209-231. University of Arizona: Mayfield Publishing Co., 1986.

Weinberg, Robert. "The Relationship Between Mental Preparation Strategies and Motor Performance: A Review and Critique." *Quest* 33 (1982): 195-213.

Wollman, Neil. "Research on Imagery and Motor Performance: Three Methodological Suggestions." *Journal of Sport Psychology* 8 (1986): 135-138.

Woolfolk, Robert, Shane Murphy, David Gottesfeld, and David Aitken. "Effects of Mental Rehearsal of Task Motor Activity and Mental Depiction of Task Outcome on Motor Skill Performance." *Journal of Sport Psychology* 7 (1985): 191-197.

Zecker, S. G. "Experimental Error or Alternative Interpretation: A Response to Ryan." *Journal of Sport Psychology* 5 (1983) 111-115.

INDEX